Edible Wild Plants:

Useful Tips About Seasonal Foraging

Table of Contents

Introduction: Everywhere you Look

Back in 2003, I can remember a certain camping trip that I went on in a large forest reserve o the East Coast. At that point in my life, my experience of foraging in the wilderness had been simply the occasional berry picking, and mushroom gathering. But when I showed up at this outing, I found myself surrounded by some expert foragers and these guys managed to drive it home to me just how enriching foraging can be. They showed me just what kind of magic can be found in the forest.

Thanks to my newfound friends I began to become intensely focused on the plat life that I was surrounded with and the possible benefits that they could provide for my diet. I mean, we weren't forced to forage because we were going to starve to death, I had packed beans and bread to last me for weeks, but it was just invigorating to pick things fresh right out of the ground.

People are generally amazed at the amount of edible food that surrounds them when it is just pointed out. In industrialized nations we are used to eating the things that have been long prepackaged on store shelves and are generally at a loss when it comes to procuring these fooods on our own. But when you can learn to grab some of these foods up—literally by the roots—then you will know how you can store and consume some of the healthiest foods known to man.

Store-bought veggies are grown more for surface aesthetics such as shape, texture, and color to entice the shopper, rather than actual nutritional value. And the process of packaging further diminishes the value of the produce as well. But when you consume veggies and plants picked right out of the ground, you are getting the best possible nutrition and value you could ever come by.

These edible plants are invaluable during a backpacking adventure as a means of extending resources and helping to boost the health of those involved on your outdoor excursion. So keep a look out folks, because when you are making a trek in the great beyond to forage, there is a little bit of magic everywhere you look.

Chapter 1: Foraging the first Fruits of Spring

As the winter months turn into spring, you will find yourself in the best time to forage. Many wild foods are taking this time to pop out of the ground, you just have to know where and what to look for. This chapter explains to you what some of the first spring-time foods to forage are, and how you can find them.

Hawthorn

Right when it starts to get warm, Hawthorn leaves can be seen beginning to form. These leaves can serve as a delicious salad. They can also be used boiled in tea for just an extra kick of flavor. Hawthorn also grows some berries that are safe to consume as well. These bright red berries are delicious and shouldn't be missed. These plants are most recognizable however by their beautiful white flowers.

As soon as you see these flowers poking up out of the ground get ready to forage for your Hawthorn leaves folks. I usually gather as much of this plant as I can and then dry them out in the sun. These dried leaves I can then later use in a wide variety of foods. Hawthorn is a good find because it has a lot of great health benefits. Hawthorn is known to help lower blood pressure and regular use has even been shown to correct an irregular heart beat.

Stinging Nettle

Much the same as Hawthorn, the leaves of the Stinging Nettle plant are good to eat and rich in nutritional value. During the spring-time months this plant's shoots grow as much as 6 inches tall, so they are fairly easy to spot. These forage items are fairly easy to obtain, scour the ground this spring until you find it. Stinging nettle has quite a few healthy benefits.

It works as a natural anti-histamine and is of great benefit during the allergy season. But it also has a good dose of serotonin, which can help boost your mood considerably when consumed. When boiled in a pot of tea, this plant also serves as an excellent diuretic. All good reasons to forage this plant! The easiest thing to do is to store the fresh leaves of the plant in a large plastic bag and seal them tightly for later use. I usually make at least 2 or three bags of these plants per foraging expedition.

Burdock

Both a healing herb and an edible plant Burdock runs the gamut. Every part of this plant is edible from top to bottom. The roots are great as a stir fry vegetable, and the flowers are good in stews and soups. The leaves are can be consumed as well, but some have complained of a slightly bitter taste from them. Nevertheless this is a good plant to forage. So keep a look out for its purple flowers when spring comes around.

But even if you don't look for this plant, chances are it will find you. If you are walking through the forest during the spring months all you have to do is look down at your shoes and pant leg and you very well might find pieces of the burdock plant attached to them in the form of spurs.

These pesky little spurs attach to people and animals in their journey of pollinating the forest, so one way or another you will encounter burdock. These plants are tasty and good for your health. Studies have shown that steady consumption of this plant can greatly enhance your immune system and aid in combating cold, flu, and allergy symptoms. This is a great asset to have on hand.

Dandelion

These hardy weeds sprout up like magic no matter what every single April, and by May you can find them all over the place. Although the Dandelion is the absolute bane of the gardener, these plants can actually be quite a nutritious food source. They work well boiled into a soup and they also taste great in roughage salads.

You can eat the stems, leaves, and flower. This plant is most definitely edible. They are also loaded with Beta Carotene, Vitamin C, Vitamin A, iron, calcium, magnesium, zinc, phosphorous, and even potassium. This heavy vitamin and mineral supply can aid in many aspects of our health. So give it a try!

Gooseberries

You can see their grey branches and bright red thorns in just about any forest in North America. The berries of this edible plant are ripe and ready to go by spring. They are called Gooseberries because of the fact that they are a favorite food source for Canadian Geese. These birds absolutely love these berries. Some humans however, have reported that the berries have a slightly bitter taste. This seems to be primarily just a matter of personal preference however, and I have never had any problem with the taste.

Coltsfoot

This edible plant grows in a wide variety of forests all throughout North America. This highly nutritious plant is easy to find growing in patches in open glades and at the entrance of wooded areas. This plant is often easily mistaken for a sunflower with its large yellow flowering which is very similar in appearance.

This plant can be eaten raw or cooked. I usually stir fry this wild veggie in order to get the most flavor and taste. Coltsfoot has a lot of health benefits, especially when it comes to aiding the respiratory system. Studies have shown that this plant can work to alleviate ailments such as asthma and bronchitis.

Cattails

Thee wild edibles are usually found at the edge of water sources such as ponds, rivers and lakes. They are found at the edges of many forests and clearings. The plant is long and slender, usually reaching a few feet tall and about 1 or 2 inches thick. The roots are dense and fibrous. Just pull this plant up by the root and fold them for storage.

Unravel them when you wish to prepare them and cook them up right in your pot. The plant can be eaten in its entirety so there is no need for waste. This plant has many well known health benefits, such as aiding in digestion and even blood circulation. So next time that you are in the forest foraging, go ahead and give the old cattail a try! You'll be glad you did!

Chapter 2: Foraging During the Summer

There are many good foods to forage during the summer months; here are a few of the best. Gather up as much of these edible plants as you can.

Blueberries

Yes, blueberries grow in the wild! They are actually quite ubiquitous in the summer months if you just know where to look. They tend to grow in meadow soil and are prevalent in Northern Europe and North America. You will most likely find blueberries growing in wooded areas, but sometimes they grow by themselves as well, and a blueberry patch has been known to spontaneously sprout up in a homeowner's back yard from time to time. This is by far my favorite food to forage. Just make sure you rinse them off before you eat them; but otherwise this wild food is fully ready to be foraged!

Strawberries

Strawberries tend to grow in fields but are also found in the woods as well. Really just any open area in the countryside could have some strawberry patches growing out of them. Strawberries are in bloom at the end of May and are in full swing by July. The first hint of strawberries beginning to grow is the telltale white strawberry flowers which start appearing in clusters right at the beginning of summer. This foraged food looks just like their store-bought counterparts, except perhaps not quite as large. They go well served by themselves or with other food. Just wash them and prep them for consumption beforehand.

Violets

They present themselves as nice flower but they can also provide for a nice snack as well. There is no part of this plant that can't be consumed. Take it whole or chop it up in a roughage salad, this plant makes for a good meal. It's also good for you since Violets are naturally rich in Vitamin C, and Vitamin A, helping to boost your health as you eat. These violets taste well cooked or raw. I usually stir fry the stems ad leaves of the plant, when eaten with rice it makes for a pretty good meal.

Chapter 3: Foraging in the Forest During the Fall

Many of us enjoy the fall. We admire the changing colors of the leaves on the trees and we relish the relief we get from hot summer days finally beginning to decrease. There are also a lot of good edible plants that can be eaten in the forest. Here are a few of the best of them.

Mustard Seed Plant

During the early days of October you can see Mustard Seed Plants sprouting right up in the forest. In any glade or opening in the forest you can find patches of these mustard seed plants growing where the sunlight hits. But before you even see them, you will most likely smell them! These plants give off an aroma that is hard to miss. After taking in a good whiff of it, you will always remember the scent.

Mustard plants have whitish-yellow flowers with four petals each. These flowers are a rather prominent feature, but it is of course the seeds that you are going to want to eat, and these can be found locked inside a heart-shaped seedpod. Mustard seed can be cooked or eaten raw.

These seeds can also be refined into mustard sauce if you have the time and patience for the enterprise. I can remember making a sizeable amount of mustard from these seeds once, so much so that I could actually sell them at the farmer's market for a profit. Not bad for something you can gather completely for free!

Wild Acorns

As well as falling leaves, the autumn months of the forest also bring falling acorns. These edible plants are a real treat that nature naturally provides for us. You can find them scattered all over the forest floor, just pick them up and collect them in a bag or basket When you are ready to eat the acorns wash them off with cool water and break their shells open.

Acorns are completely edible raw, or you could cook them. By grounding them down into powder they even work as a good kind of flour and can be used to make bread and other baked goods. The nuts themselves are best when they are freshly fallen from the trees, because if you pick them from the tree limb too soon they might not be ripe enough.

Shamrocks

Its your lucky day when you find these shamrocks because these plants are completely edible. This classic plant associated most with Leprechaun's and St. Patrick's Day just so happens to go great in soups and salads. You can usually find these guys right on the forest floor growing about 7 inches in height reaching up to the sun as it beats down through the trees.

When you spot these guys in the woods usually you will find them with whitish-pink flowering. These light pink flowers usually disappear after the plants have been in bloom a couple of weeks, but shamrocks themselves are good to head anytime. So go ahead and grab up a batch for your own lucky lettuce.

Hops

This edible pant is widely used in beer-based beverages. A native of Europe, it is a strong and potent plant. They grow thick in many forests during the months of fall. You can see them by taking note of their stout roots on the forest floor and their thick, protruding, and hairy stems. They have cone-shaped flowers with heart-shaped leaves that reach up in bundles as high as 18 feet.

Just grab up as many as you can and boil them in a pot. You can also use this edible plant to make tea. A hopped up brew of tea never hurt anybody! In fact it could greatly help you! These kinds of beverages have been known to greatly reduce inflammation from arthritis and other ailments when consumed. So be sure to have some hops in your foraged supply.

Miner's Lettuce

Just look at the green and leafy material on this plant. It's just calling for you to eat it! The leaves are perfect for salad and are always rich in vitamins and minerals. When you are camping out in the woods a salad composed of this leafy material is a refreshing respite in the forest. Miner's Lettuce is also known as Indian Lettuce and is common in the coastal forests of North America, and Canada. The leaves grow rather quickly and blanket the forest floor.

The reason why it became known as "Miner's Lettuce" is because during the gold rush in these regions, it was believed that miner's often ate the plant for its various health benefits; but most especially to prevent scurvy. Some of the other benefits are its ability to improve blood circulation, and reduce cholesterol. The lettuce comes with whitish pink flowering, usually displaying five petals. And it can be cooked or eaten raw. Miner's lettuce is a favorite topping on many good burgers and sandwiches and is a tasty and healthy alternative to store bought lettuce.

Tree collards

The word collard actually comes from "colewort" which is another name for cabbage. This edible tree cabbage is quite prevalent in the forest environment provides a constant source of leafy greens all throughout the year. These plants are delicious as well as nutritious, providing you with essential vitamins and minerals. This plant is pretty tender, so take care. But general reparation of this plant is pretty easy too. Just rinse it off with water and either eat it raw or cooked.

Blackberries

Some wild berries are risky to consume, but you shouldn't have any problem with blackberries. These blackberries can be easily spotted with their bright red stems. Just be careful when you pick these berries because thorns are usually attached. It might be best to wear gloves when picking them. The berries are at their ripest point in early September.

I usually start my rounds on the last day of October (October 31st) to find these little guys. These berries are good for you because they are loaded with Vitamin C and bioflavonoids. Blackberries serve to strengthen immune defenses and the also aid cognitive function, improving memory and concentration. Be sure to forage this wild plant when you get the chance!

Purslane

Purslane originally hails from the Arab World but in the intervening centuries it has come to inhabit every other corner of the globe as well. This edible plant can now be found growing in just about any wooded area you encounter. It tends to grow in a flattened formation and spreads rapidly in area.

This plant is easily recognized by its circular leaf structure and the large reddish stems at the plant's bottom. It is the stems that are the most nutritious part of the plant. Just one stem is full of Vitamin E, Vitamin A, Omega 3, and Calcium. It also has a good amount of phosphorous, which is all good for your general health. And all great reasons to forage this food.

Chapter 4: Wintertime Foraging in the Forest

The forest is a majestic place in the winter, the snow covers the trees and streams and ponds are frozen over as the quiet chill of winter prevails. Most figure they would have to wait until spring to forage, but this is not the case. Tehre are in fact, all kinds of foods that you can safely forage in the wintry forest. Here are some good examples.

Wild Wintergreen

Just as the name might imply this wild plant feels right at home during the wintertime months. You can usually find winter green bunched up on the forest floor, and also in the more hilly parts of a forest. This edible plant can be eaten raw or it can be boiled and eaten in soups and stews. In its dried out form its also often used as Christmas decorations, usually a classic staple at my house over the holidays. And if you chew gum you are probably well aware of its role in that field as well! Wintergreen is a natural refresher so feel free to forage it!

Oyster Mushrooms

These tasty little buddies really don't mind the cold; they sprout up just fine snow or shine! As you can see from the illustration above, they are also quite common in the forest and you can find them growing right from the base of a tree. But if you don't readily see them growing from trees, it doesn't mean they are there. You might just have to look a little bit closer.

Because one of the easiest ways to forage for these mushrooms is to grab up a piece of brush and look underneath it, these mushrooms are often found stuck right to the bottom of dead and decaying wood. The mushrooms have your typically mushroom appearance with the white caps, and grey bodies. These shrooms taste great raw or cooked.

Chickweed

Chickweed flowers can be found poking up through the snowy forest floor during most of the winter months. You will most likely find these edible plants growing in forest clearing. Sometimes however, grow in open paths and trails. You can see this flower poking up just about anywhere. This food can be eaten raw or even stir fried in a pan. You will love it. Forage as much of this edible plant as you can.

Chapter 5: Edible Plants you can Forage All Year Long

The foods presented in this chapter are good all year long, known as "perennial vegetables" these edible plants can be foraged any time of the year.

**Sweet Potatoes**

Sweet potatoes; makes me think of all those holidays with the family eating sweet potato pie and candied yams. But you mean to tell me there are sweet potatoes growing out there in the wilderness all by themselves, just waiting for me to forage them? The answer is; yes! In any rich soil environment with plenty of sunlight coming through the trees, you can find this edible plant.

The leaves of this plant are safe to consume, but of course it is the potato rooted into the ground that most would like to have for dinner. These potatoes are usually yellowish-orange and medium sized. This plant needs regular sunshine and moist soil in order to grow, so you typically find them in regions with a lot of regular rain.

Ground Plum

Find this edible plant anytime, anywhere. The Ground Plum grows on the forest floor in patches that are about 25 centimeters in height. The plum grows out of a pod. Just pluck it right from the pod. That's about it. This edible plant grows rather rapidly and doesn't require any extra effort other than plucking them and putting them in your mouth. Easy enough right? Just gather up as much of these guys as you can and enjoy them.

Garlic

I love garlic and the bulb of this edible plant is quite unmistakable, and as soon as you see it poking out of forest you can requisition it for your consumption. Garlic's taste great and have numerous health benefits, it can be rubbed into the skin as a disinfectant and it can be eaten as a means to boost the immune system. This edible plant has even been known to fight off severe illness, so be sure to forage it when you see it. Once collected you can boil it chopped with other food or even grounded into powder and sprinkled over your meals. It works great every time.

Egyptian Onion

Did you know that onions grow wild? Not only that these edible onions grow all year long! Just look out for their tall stalks and you can pick these guys right out of the forest. The actual onion itself will be found growing on top of this stalk. These plants tend to grow in forests with rather sandy soil. The bulb always sprouts on top and causes the plant to bend, creating its iconic appearance.

The bulb will eventually drop down and cause a whole new plant to bloom. It is for this reason that they are sometimes referred to as "walking onions" because they appear to walk across the field as the bulbs drop. Just pull these bulbs off and either eat them raw in your salads, and sandwiches or cook them up for a special treat.

Horseradish

This edible plant is related to the mustard seeds mentioned earlier, but unlike the seasonal focused plant of mustard seeds, horseradish can grow all year round no matter what the season brings. This edible plant matures rapidly, so you don't have to wait very long to forage it. Horseradish brings a bit of pizzazz to any meal and you will just love the taste when it is picked up fresh.

Along with the flavor this plant brings, it also brings some health benefits as well, helping to clear up nasal passages and aiding other respiratory issues by eating, and sometimes even just smelling it. It's always a great food to forage so keep on the look out for. Forage this edible plant whenever you are in the forest.

Groundnut

This edible plant is delicious and can be found growing right off the vine in just about any forest environment. The plant also regularly produces beans all year long. This edible can found hanging right off the trees of the forest. They are easy to locate because of the bright yellow flowering that emerges on the plant. This plant is grown year round but is more prevalent in autumn. Groundnut can be eaten completely raw or can be cooked. I usually like to roast mine over an open fire as I enjoy my trip in the great outdoors.

Rhubarb

It is the stalk of the rhubarb plant that tastes so good, and it is for this reason that rhubarb is used in the classic desert dish of Rhubarb Pie so often. This edible plant grows in large patches throughout the forest. It most easily stands out due to the bright red colorings of their stalks. The stalk is what you should eat. Leave the leaves alone however, as they are somewhat poisonous. Just cut off the stalks and boil them all under high heat and you have a delicious meal on your hands.

Asparagus

They can be found growing right in the middle of the forest to heights of as much as 10 inches high, just about any time of the year. These edible plants to require an adequate amount of sunlight however so you most likely won't find them in the deep dark, thick of the forest, but you will spot them at the entrance, and in clearings. Look for these patches of Asparagus all throughout the year. They make for a good addition to any part of your diet.

Globe Artichoke

This wild plant has a lot of tenacity. It can grow anywhere and anytime, producing significantly large globe artichokes. They grow as much as 6 feet and have beautiful purple and green leaves that they show off throughout the year. Rinse the plants off well when you find them and store them in large plastic bags.

This edible plant is good for any backpacking adventure that you partake in. It is also good for your health and studies have shown that eating this wilderness veggie can boost the immune system, improve blood circulation, raise mental cognition, and even aid in digestion. Not bad for something you just grabbed off the hiking trail!

Conclusion: Just Eat It!

As mentioned in this book, there are many good reasons why you should forage. One of the best reasons is your health. There are so many benefits that can be derived from these foraged foods that it is nearly impossible to put it all in the same place. We've tried our best in this book to present them to you, but even here, it doesn't quite do it justice. It can't, because the truth is, new edible plants are just now being discovered.

It is nearly an every day occurrence to find a brand new plant that carries a wide array of benefits from consumption. So when you are making your trips out to the forest environment, don't be afraid to experiment, if something appears good to you (as long as you take steps to make sure it is not toxic of course) then just eat it! Thank you for reading this book!

FREE Bonus Reminder

If you have not grabbed it yet, please go ahead and download your special bonus report *"DIY Projects. 13 Useful & Easy To Make DIY Projects To Save Money & Improve Your Home!"*
Simply Click the Button Below

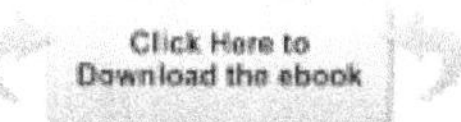

OR **Go to This Page**
http://diyhomecraft.com/free

BONUS #2: More Free & Discounted Books or Products
Do you want to receive more Free/Discounted Books or Products?
We have a mailing list where we send out our new Books or Products when they go free or with a discount on Amazon. Click on the link below to sign up for Free & Discount Book & Product Promotions.
=> Sign Up for Free & Discount Book & Product Promotions <=

OR Go to this URL
http://bit.ly/1WBb1Ek